IMAGES
of England

EPPING

Epping
Urban District Council.
1905-06

These fourteen men were Epping's local councillors in 1905/06. The Urban District Council became part of the Epping Forest District Council in 1974. (EFDM: photographs by Scott Galloway)

IMAGES
of England

EPPING

Compiled by
Sue Davies

TEMPUS

First published 1999
Copyright © Sue Davies, 1999

Tempus Publishing Limited
The Mill, Brimscombe Port,
Stroud, Gloucestershire, GL5 2QG

ISBN 0 7524 1500 X

Typesetting and origination by
Tempus Publishing Limited
Printed in Great Britain by
Midway Clark Printing, Wiltshire

A postcard from around 1900. The photographer was standing on the corner of St John's Road looking towards Station Road, which is on the left. (EFDM)

Contents

Acknowledgements

As Museum Officer at the Epping Forest District Museum I have been in the happy position of being able to select the best images from our photographic archive, which is where most of the images in this book came from. A community museum cannot exist without the support of local people and I would like to thank everyone who has donated material to the museum. A second thank-you is due to the many photographers who, over the years, have captured the images in this book. I have done my best to credit the photographer where his or her name is known. One of the aims of a museum like ours is to show material to a wide audience and we are pleased that Tempus Publishing have helped us to do so by producing this book.

A book like this is never the work of one person and I am grateful for the help I had in compiling it. Particular thanks are also due to the following organizations and people, who helped fill in gaps in my knowledge, lent their own photographs and corrected my captions:

Trevor Ambrose
Stan Barlow
Allan Church
The Corporation of London
Anne Quade
Lisa Drake
The Epping Society
Jack Farmer
Paul Flack
Catherine Foster
The Francis Frith Collection, Salisbury, Wilts, SP3 5QP
John Hamilton
Jane
London Transport Museum
Patricia Moxey
Kay Ross
Ray Sears
John Smith
The West Essex Gazette

Introduction

There has been a settlement in Epping for at least a thousand years. A market was established in Epping during the thirteenth century and, due to its location on the main road, the town grew. Many travellers passed through the town including, during the seventeenth century, the diarist Samuel Pepys who later wrote of highway robbers in Epping Forest. The early nineteenth century was the heyday of coaches. In those days up to twenty-five coaches a day would stop in Epping to change horses and refresh the travellers. As the railway replaced coaches the town suffered a little until, in 1865, a station opened. Epping's location in the Forest and its links to neighbouring towns have always been important to the residents and because of this you will find images of places like Theydon Bois, Loughton and Buckhurst Hill included in this book.

The photographs date from the 1870s to the 1970s. Many changes took place during this time. Two of Epping's best known landmarks were built: the water tower in 1872 and St John's church tower, completed in 1907. Other, less noticeable changes also occurred during this period: for example, in the late 1920s electricity first came to the High Street, Epping's cinema came (and went) and in 1969/70 the High Street was renumbered.

Despite these changes the area is still recognizable. Many buildings shown are still standing and, while there are more cars, the roads still follow the same routes. The people in the pictures also offer a sense of continuity – their clothes may differ but these images show them working, celebrating and shopping, as we do today.

Sue Davies
Epping Forest District Museum Officer
November 1998

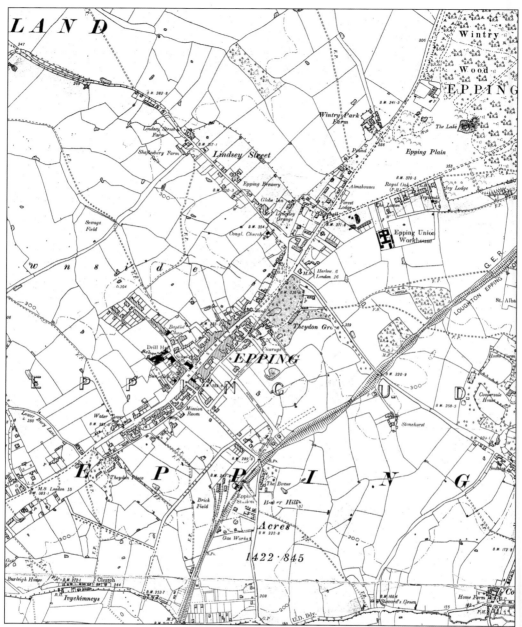

An 1897 map of Epping. The shape of the town is much the same as it is today and many familiar landmarks can be seen on this map, including the railway, the Epping Union Workhouse (now St Margaret's Hospital) and the water tower. (EFDM)

8

One
Work

Brickmakers in Buckhurst Hill in 1925. A 1922 Kelly's Directory lists William and Charles French as brickmakers based in Lower Queens Road and Epping New Road. (EFDM)

The Cottis brickworks, which were located next to Epping station, in 1899. The brickworks were established around 1890 and operated until 1937. During this time many local buildings were constructed using Cottis bricks. (EFDM)

Foundations being laid at St John's church in 1907, when extensions were made to the existing building. (EFDM)

Work in progress on St John's church tower in 1907. A seventy-eight-year-old man died while he was helping to build the tower. A memorial has been cut into the stone of the tower and can be seen today. (EFDM)

During 1906 and 1907 a new tower was added to St John's church in Epping. The vicar, Revd Allwork, poses with the workmen in this photograph. (EFDM)

At work in Nunn's the blacksmiths, September 1964. The smithy was located in Hemnall Street. (Reproduced with thanks to Allan Church)

Nunn's smithy building in May 1971, shortly before it was demolished. (EFDM)

Nunn's dairy cart. In the days before milk bottles, milk was delivered to the door and measured into the householders' jugs. (EFDM)

The Epping Co-op bakers with their delivery cart in the early 1900s. When the Co-op first opened in Epping in 1894, it was on the site now used by Lathams. This photograph was taken on that site. (EFDM)

'Billy' Prentice was known as the 'midnight baker' because he delivered bread at all hours. He is standing outside his shop in Epping High Street, opposite the Duke of Wellington public house. (EFDM)

The baker George Hummerston delivering bread with his dog, Jack. He is seen here outside the Bell in around 1905. (EFDM)

EPG.21F.   Charcoal Burning. Epping.

Between 1936 and 1942 there was an attempt to revive the ancient industry of charcoal burning in Epping Forest. This photograph probably dates from then. (Courtesy of the Francis Frith Collection)

Epping Forest woodmen in the 1920s. These men were employed by the Corporation of London to chop down overgrown trees and to thin out dense areas of forest. (EFDM)

Charcoal burning in Epping Forest at the Cuckoo Pits. This was an experiment which took place over six weeks in the autumn of 1908. The Corporation of London paid Mr Cook and Mr Bowlte (in the centre of this picture) to carry out the charcoal burning. The following year more burning took place but the enterprise was not a financial success. (EFDM)

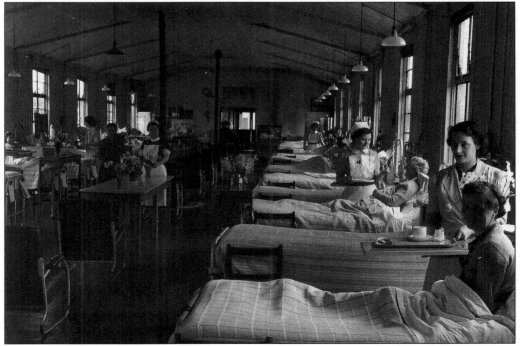

Inside one of the wards of St Margaret's Hospital in Epping around 1948. The hospital was built around Epping's workhouse and infirmary which opened in 1837. (EFDM)

Epping volunteer fire brigade in Station Road, c. 1913. The horses and pump were kept in Flack's garage. Today the building is used as a paint shop. (EFDM)

Epping fire brigade some time between 1911 and 1913, when David C. Poulton was the Chief Fire Officer. Part of the water tower is just visible in the background. (Reproduced with thanks to Jack Farmer)

Epping auxiliary fire service in 1940. From left to right: Bert Hyde, Cyril Hyde, Dennis Godfrey, Harvey Tredgett, Arthur Hyde, Bill Osborne, Fred Glasscock and Dick Glasscock. (Reproduced with thanks to Jack Farmer)

This postcard from around 1902 shows Loughton post office with St Mary's church in the background. (EFDM)

The staff of Epping post office in 1904. The postmaster, Mr Sibley, sits in the centre. Epping post office has moved location several times. This photograph dates from the time when the post office was on the corner of Station Road and the High Street. (EFDM)

Post Office Corner at the top of Station Road, Epping. The building, dated 1898, was the post office for a number of years. It still stands in a modified form. (EFDM)

The printers and stationery shop of Alfred B. Davies in Loughton. An enterprising man, he produced local postcards, some of which are reproduced in this book. He also had a shop in the Victoria buildings in Epping. (EFDM)

Built in the 1870s as an iron foundry, work continued at W. Cottis's works until 1982. The building, known as the Archimedean Ironworks, was located just behind the High Street, but was later demolished. Offices now occupy the site. (EFDM)

Jack Watts inside the agricultural store of W. Cottis & Sons in 1950. He was employed by them from 1935 until 1962. (EFDM)

Staff of William Cottis & Sons, Epping, in around 1948. Cottis were well known for making agricultural tools and machinery. (EFDM)

On 5 April 1969 a fire swept through the old Cottis premises, destroying much of the agricultural stock. Donald Denoon Motors had taken the premises over from Cottis in the early 1960s. (EFDM)

Rose Salaun making sausages at Church's butchers in January 1952. Epping sausages have long had a reputation for excellence. This is probably due, in part, to the long established rights of local people to let their pigs graze in the Forest, which meant that it was relatively cheap to raise pigs. (Reproduced with thanks to Allan Church)

Two
Schools

A class at Theydon Garnon School in 1907. (EFDM)

The cricket team of Theydon Garnon School in 1907. The team played five matches that season and won three. (EFDM)

Theydon Garnon School in 1945. The school building has since been converted to a private residence. (EFDM)

Theydon Garnon School in 1945. Some of these pupils look as if they have dressed up in 'costumes from around the world'! (EFDM)

'Swedish Drill' at Theydon Garnon School. At the time this photograph was taken, the headmaster was G.H. Lemon. A new building for the school was funded in 1850 by Miss Harriet Archer-Houblon, who lived in Coopersale. (EFDM)

Epping and Theydon Garnon Boys' School, *c.* 1910. (EFDM)

A class at Theydon Bois School in 1923. The school was established in 1840 and enlarged in 1903. At the time of this photograph about 155 children attended the school under the direction of Miss Emily Glover. (EFDM)

The Quakers, or Society of Friends, ran a school on the site marked by the cross. The school ceased to function in 1874 and the building was demolished. The building in the photograph was built in the late Edwardian period; today it forms part of the Epping Forest District Council's offices. (EFDM)

A group of children from St John's Infants' School, Epping, in 1928. The building used by the infants' school at this time was destroyed by a bomb in 1940. The site of the old building is now a playground. (Reproduced with thanks to Allan Church)

A class at St John's Primary School, Epping, in 1902. St John's School has since moved to a different building; the old school, seen here, is now used as a centre for adult and community education. (EFDM)

Staples Road School, Loughton, in 1920. Staples Road School for Boys opened in 1888 with 366 pupils. An infants' school was added in 1892 and in 1911 the junior school expanded, creating 316 places for girls. (EFDM: photograph by R.H. Wickens)

A postcard of Loughton School for Boys, sent in 1907. (EFDM)

Loughton High School for Girls, on Alderton Hill, in 1938. This school first opened in 1908. (EFDM)

Three
Transport

A group of people watch the 'Aerial Derby' above St John's church tower. The event was organized by the *Daily Mail* newspaper between 1912 and 1914. The pilots had to pass over Epping in their 95-mile circuit around London. Orville and Wilbur Wright's famous first flight had taken place only ten years earlier so aircraft were still a novel sight. (EFDM)

A penny-farthing in Epping High Street. The George and Dragon (now the Forest and Firkin) is in the background. The penny-farthing had a brief life. Models were first made in 1870 and it went out of production in 1892, replaced by designs more like modern bicycles. (EFDM)

A messenger from Epping post office in 1907. (EFDM)

The real heyday of coaching was long over when this photograph was taken in 1907. The *Alderman Roll* coach, here seen standing outside the Cock public house in Epping, was run by Alderman James Roll of Wanstead, who was a coaching enthusiast. It travelled between the Eagle in Snaresbrook and the Green Man in Harlow. (EFDM)

A group of men look ready for a good day out during the 1910s. They are standing in front of Dearlove's shop which is now 225 High Street. (EFDM)

A bus, on hire from the Vanguard fleet, standing outside the Bell Inn in Epping around 1909. (EFDM)

An accident on the Epping Road in 1915. It is difficult to see how this bus ended up on its side but it must have been a bumpy ride! (Reproduced with thanks to the London Transport Museum)

James Peppitt worked as a chauffeur, car mechanic and bicycle repairer for the Cottis family. He is seen here in around 1910. (EFDM)

An accident in Theydon Bois involving a car belonging to one of the Buxton family. It appears to be a head-on collision but both drivers seem unscathed. In the early twentieth century vehicles like these travelled at low speeds. (EFDM)

A puncture undergoing repair in Epping High Street in the early 1900s. (EFDM)

The 'Epping Auto-Shunter' seems to have been an experimental vehicle made in the 1950s. It was a petrol-driven tractor able to drive over rails and move stationary trains. (EFDM)

A postcard of Epping station sent in 1912. The railway came to Epping in 1865 when the Eastern Counties Railway extended the line from Loughton to Epping and Ongar. (EFDM)

Tube trains powered by electricity first came to Epping in the late 1940s but they did not entirely replace steam trains for some years. This is the last steam train to leave Epping station, on 18 November 1957. (Reproduced with thanks to the London Transport Museum)

Buckhurst Hill station staff, around 1883. The coming of the railway resulted in many houses being built in Buckhurst Hill during the second half of the nineteenth century. (EFDM)

Buckhurst Hill station, c. 1905. (EFDM)

Loughton station during the late 1920s. The sweeping shape of the platform is still very recognizable today. (EFDM)

Loughton station staff around 1906. The railway came to Loughton in 1856, nine years before the line reached Epping. (EFDM)

Four
Special Events

The circus comes to Epping in 1880. Elephants in the High Street were an unusual sight then (as they would be now!). (EFDM)

The funeral of Robert Marriott in July 1899. The deceased man was a member of the Epping Town Band, who are playing as the funeral party walks along the High Street towards the cemetery at Epping Upland. (EFDM)

Joseph Hills, the Epping grocer, poses with his cart which has been decorated for the coronation of Edward VII, August 1902. The coronation was delayed by six weeks because the King had to undergo an appendicitis operation. (EFDM)

A band playing outside the George and Dragon, around 1895. The pub still exists, but has been renamed: today it is known as the Forest and Firkin. (Reproduced thanks to Allan Church)

The results of the election of Epping's MP being announced outside the old police station on 25 January 1910. The successful candidate was Col. Lockwood, who later became Lord Lambourne. (EFDM)

Election posters for G.E. Rush of Epping. The boys appear to be happy to campaign for Rush in this photograph. Perhaps he offered better tree-climbing rights! (EFDM)

Winston Churchill addressing a crowd
from the balcony of the Victoria buildings
in Epping High Street. Winston Churchill
served as Epping's MP from 1924 until
1945. After 1945 he took over the new
constituency of Woodford. (EFDM)

A huge bonfire in High Beach, built to
celebrate the coronation of George V in
1911. Note the air vents built in to allow
the fire to burn. (EFDM)

The 2nd Leyton Boy Scout troop at the junction of Station Road and the High Street in Epping in 1912. The troop was camping on the Copped Hall estate. (EFDM)

A wedding party outside St John's church in Epping. The bride and groom must have been cycling enthusiasts since their transport is a tandem! (EFDM)

An open day at Copped Hall during the 1920s. Copped Hall was gutted by fire in May 1917 (caused, it is thought, by a hair clip used as a fuse wire). Today the remains of the Hall still stand and the Copped Hall Trust are fighting to restore the house. (EFDM)

Inside the Congregational church some time after 1920. The Revd Locke is in the pulpit. (Reproduced with thanks to Allan Church)

A street party in James Street, Epping, held to celebrate the Silver Jubilee of George V in 1935. (EFDM)

Mrs Buxton planting an oak tree on Theydon Bois green to mark George V's Silver Jubilee in 1935. About forty trees were planted but only a few survive. (EFDM)

A group of children outside the Empire cinema in Epping. The bunting is to celebrate George V's Silver Jubilee in 1935. The Empire cinema shut in 1954 and the building still stands, although somewhat altered. (EFDM)

The army marching through Epping in 1939. The International Stores and the Victoria Buildings are visible in the background. (Reproduced with thanks to Allan Church)

A parade through Epping High Street in the early 1930s. (EFDM: photograph by Norman Smith)

The carnival queen, Edna Williams, and her attendants form part of Epping's celebrations to mark the coronation of George VI in May 1937. (EFDM)

The old folks' tea party in James Street, Epping, in 1953 to mark Elizabeth II's accession to the throne. (EFDM)

A street party to celebrate the 1953 Coronation in James Street, Epping. (EFDM)

Another celebration showing the coronation parade. (EFDM)

Prize-giving at Epping's celebration on 2 June 1953, the day Elizabeth II was crowned. Mrs Matthews and the Revd Matthews are presenting the prizes. (EFDM)

The same occasion as the picture above, 2 June 1953. The houses behind the float were later knocked down to make way for the Civic Offices. (EFDM)

A 1953 Coronation party for the children in James Street, Epping. (EFDM)

The opening of the Forester's new cricket pavilion, around 1966. (Reproduced with thanks to Allan Church)

Five
People

Benjamin Winstone was a worthy of Epping who wrote about the town's history. He lived in a house called Oakridge which used to stand on a site next to the Tower Garage. In 1885 he wrote a book about St John the Baptist's church in Epping. (EFDM)

The 'Cock Birds' at a charity dinner in 1938. This group of men met at the Cock Hotel, hence the name. A number of the diners are wearing fancy dress – note the fake beards! (Reproduced with thanks to Allan Church)

A group of Epping ladies, including Mrs Doe and Mrs Strange, are ready for an outing in their homemade hats! This is a studio portait; the pier scene is a painted backdrop. (Reproduced with thanks to Jane)

The Church family with billeted soldiers, outside their house, The Homestead, in Epping, 23 April 1915. The site was later used by Unigate Dairies and is now used by the Epping Forest District Council. (Reproduced with thanks to Allan Church)

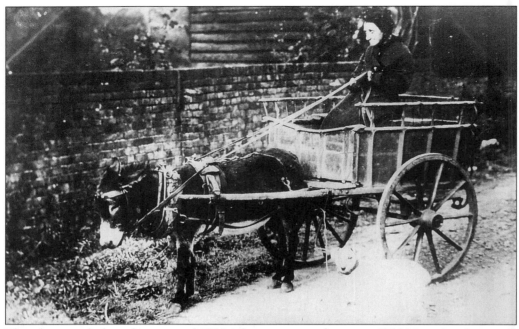

This photograph dates from around 1900. The woman was known as 'Old Moggy' and was well known around Epping. She made her living selling eggs. She died in 1905. (EFDM)

Reuben Cottis (1840-1923). This photograph, like the one opposite, was taken in the late 1870s or 1880s, a time when many people, if they could afford it, visited photographic studios to have their portraits taken using the relatively new technology. (EFDM)

Crispus Cottis (1837-1917). With his father, William, Crispus was the driving force behind the establishment in 1858 of a blast furnace in Epping. The iron business grew and, while agricultural equipment remained at its core, this Epping business diversified to include an ironmonger's shop and a brickworks as well as a cycle and motor shop. (EFDM)

William Cottis Jnr (1838-1890) and his wife. Like his brother overleaf, William was a member of one of Epping's 'first families'. The Cottis family were prominent in the business and civic life of the town during the late nineteenth and early twentieth centuries. (EFDM)

The triumphant return to Epping from the Boer War (1899-1902) of Crispus Joseph Cottis (1870-1945) and other Epping soldiers. The party is passing in front of the old White Lion pub in Epping High Street. (EFDM)

Letters from Crispus Cottis published in *The Epping Monthly Record*, 15 August 1900. Crispus Joseph Cottis wrote regular letters home which were published in this local paper.

EPPING DISTRICT AND THE WAR.

The following letters are the latest we have received from Trooper Cris. Cottis, of the Imperial Yeomanry :—

Smaldeel, 2/7/1900.

Dear Mr. Davis,—To-day we complete six months of our service, so that we have done half our time, even if they keep us for our full 12, which I think is hardly probable. After leaving Brandfort we marched on to Vet River, and thence next day through this place on to Doorn Spruit without anything happening, though each night there were rumours of Boers. Next day, however, we went on to Zand River, and immediately after starting we could hear the big guns going, and knew we were in for some fun. We found that Zand River was being attacked by a wandering commando under De Wet, about 900 strong, with five guns. There were about 180 of us, and we had three transport wagons with us. We had to enter the place over a ridge, and immediately we showed over the top all the Boer fire was directed at us, and our reception was therefore warm, not to say sultry. Bullets were dropping all round us, and we were all pleased when we reached the cover of the railway embankment. Three of the men (none in the " Suffolks ") were wounded, one in the leg, one along the top of his head, and one slightly in the arm. One fellow fell off his horse and broke his collar bone. We were kept for patrol work for a few days, but the Boers had all cleared off, evidently mistaking our wagons for guns. Then we were sent down here, and have been doing the same sort of work here. To-day we have got orders to move up to Kroonstad and join our company to go on some flying column somewhere, and are expecting to start every minute. We haven't seen any Boers here, but I saw four of the dead ones at Zand River (they have found 24 up to date). Have just got orders to entrain (in coal trucks) in an hour, so I must wind up. Thought I would send this on from here, as later might not be in time for August *Record*. Kindest regards to all at Epping. Yours very truly,

CRIS. J. COTTIS.

Sorry to leave off in such a hurry, but military trains won't wait.

Kroonstad, 5/7/1900.

Dear Mr. Davis,—Supplementing my short note from Smaldeel. After a wet, crowded, and uncomfortable night in a coal truck, we reached this place on Tuesday morning. We came up to camp same night, but on account of the traffic we were unable to unload our horses till next day. Our camp here is on the Valsch River, in a very pleasant and handy position. We are not on the flying column after all, as most of our horses are too knocked up. We saw the column go out. It consisted of the Armstrong Battery and about 3,000 men, chiefly Queenslanders (Bushmen), with a few of the C. I. V's. and some mounted infantry. They looked a business-like lot, and should, I think, quickly pay paid to De Wet's account. We hear that four of the details of Yeomanry left at Zand River by us have been killed and several wounded, among the latter being Sergt. Ridout, of the Berkshires. This is Arthur Ridout, who will be remembered by all Epping football players as one of our backs in the Brown-Parkinson days. They say he is wounded in three places, but none are serious, fortunately. All the talk here is about going home, but I don't expect we shall leave for at least another two months. A rumour has just reached us that General Botha has been captured. We hope it is true, as it will make a lot of difference, although De Wet will never surrender, but will have to be captured. At least, that is the impression here. He is so infuriated at the destruction of his farm that he has vowed never to give in, but to fight to the bitter end. How he is going to escape from the force now after him puzzles me though. We have just had served out to us a complete change of under-clothing, which we very much wanted. We hear that heaps of money have been subscribed in England for the Yeomanry, but we get none of the comforts sent out for us. There is a big marquee at Bloemfontein crammed full of good things for us, but that seems as near as we shall get to them. It seems rather a pity that this should be so, especially as we should appreciate them so much now. Would you kindly send me a few of the latest comic songs and one or two patriotic ones which are now going? Have just been cutting the hair of one of our lieutenants, and he tells me he thinks we shall soon be ordered home. Hope so! Kindest regards to all at Epping. Hope the missing letters have reached you. Don't send songs if you hear we are ordered home.

Yours very truly, CRIS. J. COTTIS.

P.S.—William Riggs has been made a lance-corporal to-day.

Staff at Cottis' ironmongery shop around 1907. Little is known about the black man except that he was used to advertise knife polish. Dressed as a woman, he sat in the window of the shop. (EFDM)

Mrs Barlow with her sons Ted and Stan during the 1920s. They are standing outside the Golden Iris sweet shop in Epping High Street. Mr Barlow ran the Epping Barbers next door to the Golden Iris. (Reproduced with thanks to Stan Barlow)

Damage caused by a falling tree to the bakers' granary in Theydon Bois around 1915. The granary belonged to Albert Barnes, who stands here with his children Bert, Rosie and Emmie. The man in white was Mr Smith, a baker employed by Barnes. (Reproduced with thanks to Jack Farmer)

The staff of Church's butchers ready for an outing around 1955. This photograph was taken at the rear of one of the butcher's shops. The site is now occupied by the Co-op. (Photograph by Sydney Cross; reproduced with thanks to Allan Church)

Herbert Butt with his dog, Norah, in the 1920s. Herbert Butt was a forest keeper and is seen here dressed in the formal uniform of forest keepers which included a brown velvet jacket. The role of the forest keepers was to patrol Epping Forest and ensure that visitors behaved themselves. (EFDM)

Sidney Butt, a forest keeper, with his wife Louisa. She is holding their only child, Hilda, who was born in April 1904. The baby's fancy white dress would suggest that this was taken on the day she was christened. (EFDM)

A group of men enjoying a drink inside the Thatched House Hotel during the mid-1950s. The man second from the left is Harry England, who was the last workhouse master of the Epping Union. He was in charge of the institution between 1933 and 1958 during which time it became St Margaret's General Hospital. Second from the right is Alfred Simmonds, who was the workhouse master before Harry England. (Photograph by Jelly Ltd)

Hilda England, who worked as matron of St Margaret's General Hospital. Her husband was Harry England, who can be seen in the photograph above. This image was taken in the late 1950s. (Photograph by E. Jacques Burrell)

Ray Willingale, a local builder, and Ray Stebbings in Epping High Street in the 1960s. Ray Stebbings was a partner in the chemists Slaters, which has evolved into Lloyds. This photograph was an early Polaroid. (Reproduced with thanks to Allan Church)

Some of Epping's ARP (Air Raid Precautions) workers in 1939. In the background is Ivy Lodge, The Plain, which was the ARP base. (Reproduced with thanks to Allan Church)

Second World War air-raid wardens. This group, B7, was based at the vicarage in Theydon Bois. (Reproduced with thanks to Jack Farmer)

Epping's special constables in 1945 at the rear of the police station in Epping. (Photograph by E. Jacques Burrell)

Six
Fun in the Forest

Fairmead Lodge, Chingford. This was already established as a large catering venue in the mid-nineteenth century, able to seat hundreds of people at a time. The Corporation of London bought the lodge in the late nineteenth century, demolished the building and returned the site to forest land. (EFDM)

Gray's Retreat in Theydon Bois. The train brought hundreds of day trippers to Epping Forest in the late nineteenth and early twentieth centuries. This and other retreats offered entertainment and refreshments. (EFDM)

The Roseville Retreat in High Beach in 1911. Retreats began to appear during the 1870s and, as more visitors came to the Forest, they flourished during the early years of the twentieth century. (Courtesy of the Francis Frith collection)

Bartholomew's Retreat near High Beach. (EFDM)

A sign advertising Riggs' Retreat. (EFDM; Photograph by Bernard Ward)

Riggs' Retreat in Theydon Bois. The retreat was opened in 1882 and this photograph was taken early in its history. The Riggs family had two other retreats in Epping Forest: one in High Beach and another in Chingford. (EFDM)

Donkeys and carousel at Yates' retreat, Theydon Bois. (EFDM)

Turpin's Cave in High Beach. During the late nineteenth century tea rooms were built onto many pubs for day trippers who did not want alcohol. (EFDM)

Another view of Turpin's Cave in High Beach. Tradition has it that the highway man Dick Turpin had a hideout in Epping Forest. This building was demolished in 1973 and a private house now stands on this site. (EFDM)

Donkey rides in Epping Forest. The man on the right is Bob Harrington, a forest keeper who worked for the Corporation of London between 1914 and 1920. The well-dressed children on the donkeys are surrounded by poorer children who seem to be more enthusiastic about having their photograph taken. (EFDM)

A pearly pair of children at a donkey show at Birch Hall, Theydon Bois, around 1900. There still is a regular donkey derby in Theydon Bois. (EFDM)

Boxall's Tea Rooms in Lambourne End in the 1910s. The open-top bus is destined for North Woolwich. Many day trippers to the area came by public transport. (EFDM)

Abridge 'Coffee Tavern'. (EFDM)

The Acacia Café, close to Theydon Bois station, was owned by Herbert W. Chapman during the 1930s. It was run by his three daughters Amy, Ella and Mary. (Reproduced with thanks to John Smith)

An unknown group outside the Acacia Café in the 1930s. (Reproduced with thanks to John Smith)

The start of a cycle race in Epping. This postcard was printed around 1900. (Reproduced with thanks to Allan Church)

Alan Stewart in action at the High Beach Speedway around 1936. The very first speedway meeting was held at High Beach in February 1928. The Epping Forest Field Centre and Information Centre now occupy the site of the speedway track. (EFDM)

The Hunt outside the Cock in Epping, *c.* 1918. (EFDM)

The Essex Hounds at Abridge in 1916. (EFDM)

A postcard showing a crowd watching the Essex drag hunt races 1909. (EFDM)

Epping Town Football Club in the mid-1920s. The club was formed in 1888 and continued for nearly 100 years. The man in the middle row on the far right is Sid Hills, a well-known local historian. In the same row, third from the left is Leonard Flack. (Reproduced with thanks to Paul Flack)

Theydon Bois Cricket Club, 1890s. Sitting are: Jock Wiseman, Stan Griffiths, Freddie Green, Erine Wort, Tom Keen, Arthur Keen. Standing behind are: E. Bromley, Jack Halls, 'Dingy' Dawkins, R.O. Thomas, Bill Trimby, Mr Watts. (Reproduced with thanks to Jack Farmer)

Theydon Bois Cricket Club in the early 1900s. (Reproduced with thanks to Jack Farmer)

Theydon Bois Cricket Club during the 1920s. (Reproduced with thanks to Jack Farmer)

Epping cricket pavilion. Revd Buckmaster stands in the centre of this photograph, which dates from around 1900. (Reproduced with thanks to Jack Farmer)

The Epping Town Band. In the days before radios, tapes and CDs live music was very important as an everyday source of entertainment. (EFDM)

The Epping Town Band in 1897. The band had been founded three years earlier and practised on Thursday nights in the drill hall in St John's Road. (EFDM)

The swimming pool at Grange Farm Centre. Opened in the 1950s, Grange Farm was a large sports centre offering facilities for swimming, tennis and football, as well as accommodation for 400 young people. (Courtesy of the Francis Frith Collection)

The main entrance to the Grange Farm Centre in Chigwell. (Courtesy of the Francis Frith Collection)

Seven

Pubs, Hotels and Inns

The Warren Wood pub, on the Epping New Road, in the early years of the twentieth century. The hay carts were probably on their way home having delivered their goods to market in London. (EFDM)

This postcard of the King's Oak at High Beach was sent by Ruth to Ida in 1911. The building still stands and continues to operate as a pub. (EFDM)

A postcard from around 1910 showing the Robin Hood pub. The pub is still running but the roads, and traffic, have changed. (EFDM)

The Duke of Wellington pub at High Beach. On the reverse of this postcard, written in 1910, is the following: '...We have been going about each day. We have come to Chigwell today, and it is very pleasant. We have been to Epping, Ongar and Theydon.' (EFDM)

The Bell Inn, around 1908. (EFDM)

The Bell Inn in Epping in the late 1950s. The building still stands, although it has a new façade today. It has been incorporated into the Trusthouse Forte Bell Hotel. (Courtesy of the Francis Frith Collection)

The Bell in the early 1900s. The patterned plasterwork, or pargetting, remains visible today despite the modern extensions. (EFDM)

The Essex Field Club in 1891 or 1892 inside the Wake Arms. The Essex Field Club was a group of prominent local archaeologists and natural historians. (EFDM)

Large or small parties Catered for.   Meadow for Children's Parties.
Special Terms.   Seating accommodation for 300 persons.   Indoor or Out.
PERSONAL SUPERVISION BY MRS. HORACE ARNOLD.
Special Hot & Cold Luncheons and Afternoon Teas.   Free Parking for Cars.
Up-to-date Lounge

WAKE ARMS INN, EPPING FOREST, EPPING.   PROP. HORACE ARNOLD OF POPLAR.
PHONE: LOUGHTON 257.

A postcard advertising the Wake Arms Inn. This building was demolished and a new pub/restaurant was built on the site. It now operates as Old Orleans. (EFDM)

The Wake Arms roundabout in the late 1950s when the Wake Arms Inn still existed. (Courtesy of the Francis Frith Collection)

THE "FOREST GATE INN,"

The Noted Place for BEANFEASTS &
PLEASURE PARTIES.

Within 2 Minutes of EPPING FOREST.
...... 1¼ Miles from THEYDON BOIS. ......
Return Fare from London 1/4.

BELL COMMON, EPPING.

A post card advertising the Forest Gate Inn, Epping. The swings shown are no longer in place. (EFDM)

The Forest Gate Inn as it was in 1973. (Photograph by Stuart Turner. Reproduced with thanks to the Epping Society)

The White Hart pub in Epping High Street in the mid-1960s. This building was knocked down in the late 1960s. The site is now next to the espresso bar, Paninis. (Reproduced with thanks to the *West Essex Gazette*)

The George and Dragon pub in 1973. The building is still a pub but the name has changed to the Forest and Firkin. (Photograph by Stuart Turner. Reproduced with thanks to the Epping Society)

The White Swan in Epping High Street. The building was demolished in the 1960s. Today the site is occupied by the general store, Wells. (Courtesy of the Francis Frith Collection)

The Old White Swan being pulled down during the early 1920s. Another pub, called the White Swan, was built on the same site. This new White Swan can be seen in the photograph above. (Reproduced thanks to Allan Church)

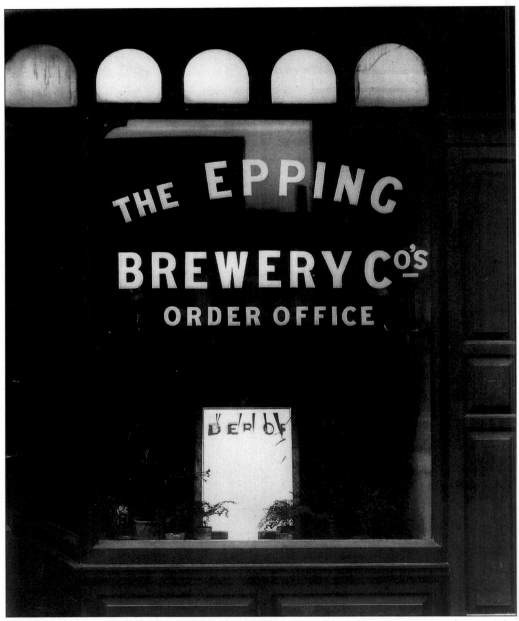

Epping Brewery in Lindsey Street. This firm produced local beer between 1840 and 1907. The building still exists today. (EFDM)

A postcard of the Cock Hotel in Epping in around 1900. The Cock was a stop for many of the coaches which passed through Epping. (EFDM)

The Maltings on Palmers Hill, Epping. The land around Epping once produced large quantities of barley. This photograph was taken by E.J.C. Courtney just before the building was demolished in 1901. (EFDM)

The Merry Fiddlers Pub, Fiddlers Hamlet, on the outskirts of Epping, in 1908. The man holding the horse's head is Cyril Church. (EFDM)

The Queen's Head pub in North Weald in the late 1950s. (Courtesy of the Francis Frith Collection)

Eight
Views of the High Street

Children around the water fountain during the early 1900s. The water fountain was erected in 1887 to mark Queen Victoria's Golden Jubilee. It was removed in 1961 and reinstated in 1989. (EFDM)

This postcard of Epping was sent in 1914 but the image is older. The trees along the High Street were planted in 1887 to celebrate Queen Victoria's Golden Jubilee. (EFDM)

The Thatched House Hotel is on the left of this view of Epping High Street in 1921. (Courtesy of the Francis Frith Collection)

Epping High Street around 1929. The Cottee garage, in the middle of this row of shops, sold bicycles and items for cars. (EFDM)

The old St John the Baptist's church in Epping. This building was demolished and replaced by the present day parish church, on the same site, in 1889. (EFDM)

An aerial view of Epping showing St John's church and the Empire cinema. This photograph was taken by Ray Stebbings between 1946 and 1954.

A view of St John's church in the late 1950s. (Courtesy of the Francis Frith Collection)

A view from the water tower. This postcard was produced by a local printer, A.B. Davis, and it was sent in 1911. (EFDM)

This aerial view of Epping shows Buttercross Lane and the fields which are today occupied by the Coronation Hill Estate. The photograph was taken by Ray Stebbings around 1956.

The High Street in the 1950s. In the foreground on the right-hand side is a petrol pump which was operated by the Cottee garage. (Courtesy of the Francis Frith Collection)

This postcard, sent in 1918, shows the Thatched House Hotel on the right and the Black Lion Pub on the left. Both are still running today. (EFDM)

A view showing the Cock Hotel on the left-hand side during the mid-1960s. (Courtesy of the Francis Frith Collection)

A view from the east end of the High Street during the early 1960s. (Courtesy of the Francis Frith Collection)

Epping's water tower was built in 1872. It was part of a wider plan to improve the sanitation in the town which, at the time, had one of the highest death rates in Essex due to the prevalence of cholera, typhoid and other water-borne diseases. (Courtesy of the Francis Frith Collection)

The old police station. This building was pulled down in November 1938. The current police station and magistrates' court was built on the same site. (Reproduced with thanks to Allan Church)

The official re-opening of Epping High Street in May 1961 after a renovation organized by the Civic Trust. (Reproduced with thanks to Allan Church)

Church Hill in 1975. These houses were demolished to make way for the Epping Forest District Council's civic offices. (Photograph by Stuart Turner. Reproduced with thanks to the Epping Society)

Nine
The Market and Shops

Epping High Street in the 1950s. (Courtesy of the Francis Frith Collection)

Market day in Epping in the 1930s. Cattle were sold at the Epping Market until 1961. (EFDM)

In the background of this market-day scene the Victoria Buildings are being constructed. The Victoria Buildings were completed in 1899. On the ground floor was a printing works, a photographic studio, a restaurant and an estate agent. Upstairs was a large hall and a number of meeting rooms. The building was demolished in the 1960s. The site is now occupied by the Co-op. (EFDM)

Market Day in Epping in the late 1920s or early 1930s. There has been a market in Epping since 1253. In the past market day was on Friday but nowadays it is held on Mondays. (EFDM)

A charity auction held in Epping High street in the early 1950s. Trevor Ambrose is at the microphone. (Reproduced with thanks to Trevor Ambrose)

A special Christmas poultry market in Epping on 16 December 1957. The farmer of the three turkeys on the table has won a prize. (Reproduced with thanks to Trevor Ambrose)

A poultry market used to be held weekly, every Monday, behind the Cock Hotel in Epping. This photograph is of a special Christmas market which was held in the old drill hall in Hemnall Street. (Reproduced with thanks to Trevor Ambrose)

A postcard produced by A.B. Davis of market day in Epping around 1903. (EFDM)

S.J. Church the butchers around 1909. This was the second Church's butchers shop to open in Epping. The site is now used by Panini's, an espresso bar. (EFDM)

Another of Church's butchers shops as it was in 1927. Aberdeen House is now incorporated into the Co-op. (EFDM)

Willingales the butchers some time during the 1920s. Willingales occupied the site now used by Barclays Bank on Epping High Street. (Reproduced with thanks to Allan Church)

Harold Hammett the butchers occupied the shop now used by Sew and Sews. (Reproduced with thanks to Allan Church)

Cottis' hardware shop and their garage during the 1940s. (EFDM)

Mallinson's was on Epping High Street near Station Road, opposite St John's church. This image is dated 1907. (EFDM)

The Epping Restaurant in 1900. It was run by George Hummerston whose family owned the property for around 200 years. (EFDM)

The ruins of the Empire cinema after a fire in May 1923. The cinema was rebuilt after the fire and the projectors were finally turned off in 1954. (Reproduced with thanks to Allan Church)

Oakley's shop, which sold boots, shoes and stuffed animals, seen here in 1923. The Empire cinema, next door, is advertising *Dick Turpin*. (Reproduced with thanks to Allan Church)

Pyne's stores in Epping High Street in the 1950s. There were two Pyne's shops in Epping, selling an array of home goods, before they closed in the mid-1990s. (EFDM)

Some kind of special event is taking place outside the Epping Stores and Dearlove's. (EFDM)

Epping Homes and Gardens (now Latham's) and Cottis Hardware (now a tile and bathroom showroom) in 1975. (Photograph by Stuart Turner. Reproduced with thanks to the Epping Society)

A.E. Batchelor's sports shop in 1973. (Photograph by Stuart Turner. Reproduced with thanks to the Epping Society)

Currys and Barclays Bank in
1975, on the same sites as
they are today. The Brunchi
Bar has been replaced by an
Indian restaurant.
(Photograph by Stuart
Turner. Reproduced with
thanks to the Epping Society)

The Epping Fruiterers in
1973. (Photograph by Stuart
Turner. Reproduced with
thanks to the Epping Society)

The International Stores in 1975. This shop was later occupied by Cullens but is currently empty. The naturalist Henry Doubleday was born in a building on this site. (Photograph by Stuart Turner. Reproduced with thanks to the Epping Society)

The shop on the corner of Epping High Street and Station Road undergoing a re-fit in 1976. (EFDM)

Ten
Views Beyond Epping High Street

A postcard sent in 1908 showing the 'convalescent cottage' by The Plain, Epping. This house has since been demolished and today the Wintery Park service station stands on this site. (Reproduced with thanks to Allan Church)

The Plain, Epping. The road to the right leads to St Margaret's Hospital and on to North Weald. Today there are mature trees on the plain. Local legend has it that an Epping resident used his walking stick to plant acorns from his garden on this patch of land! (EFDM)

EPPING: BURY LANE.

This postcard of Bury Lane was sent in 1907. (EFDM)

A postcard of Lindsey Street, Epping. (EFDM)

A postcard of St John's Road, Epping, which was sent in 1905. (EFDM)

The Black Cottage, 73 Bell Common, in 1973. This weatherboarded house still stands. (Photograph by Stuart Turner. Reproduced with thanks to the Epping Society)

Sunnyside Road, Epping, under construction around 1935. (EFDM)

Houses in Fiddlers Hamlet, next door to the Merry Fiddlers pub, 1973. (Photograph by Stuart Turner. Reproduced with thanks to the Epping Society)

Coopersale Common around 1900. The houses on the right were demolished and replaced by the Parklands estate during the 1960s. (EFDM)

Coopersale Common post office and general shop in 1960. The building is now used as a house. (EFDM)